POST-APOTHECARY

POST-APOTHECARY

SANDRA RIDLEY

PEDLAR PRESS | Toronto

ACKNOWLEDGEMENTS
The publisher wishes to thank the Canada Council for
the Arts and the Ontario Arts Council for their generous
support of our publishing program.

LIBRARY AND ARCHIVES CANADA
CATALOGUING IN PUBLICATION

Ridley, Sandra, 1973-
             Post-apothecary / Sandra Ridley.

Poems.
ISBN 978-1-897141-45-8

   I. Title.

PS8635.I344P67 2011   C811'.6
C2011-904296-7

COVER ART Holly Farrell *Apothecary Bottles*, 2008,
acrylic and oil on masonite

DESIGN Zab Design & Typography, Toronto

TYPEFACE Garamond

Printed in Canada

For N,
my constant

CONTENTS

PROLOGUE

Pulse

She is right handed, left. Retain the language not the visual side.
She is hungry. She is nil-by-mouth.

She is a note hung over a bed, a metal trolley & swinging doors.
She is semi-prone & steadied & there are nights.

An onslaught of nights. On, off, oxygen ventilation. Reeled.
Rocked. A wet tangle of hair. Her hand swept over a bright eye.

She is making it all up.
Can't possibly see through a retinal slit, out the dilated corner of.

REST
CURE

Sun
light.
    Light
light light light.

Denise Levertov

i.

Before running on nightshade & wormwood in a topiary maze.

Before hawthorn punctures her arm — poison tipped.

Before a peck of stones, she handpicks or pockets,
she is camphor-doused
& blinded
by a fold of wool — wet & held tight to her eyes.

Before his screen & clips & the red light & darkening, his hands pressed
forward
to his switchboard
& mirror — apparatus of the in-out & charged.

Before her fluoroscopic diapositive &
the smell of two kinds of heat.

      Nothing left hidden in her body.

Before & after, there is only this — four corners to a room
& the others pounding at the door.

ii.

Corset unstrung,
she frets — swirled thick &
unfit
on plum cordial &
her wish for nothing but a tumbler of cold water.

      Fog wiped from a looking glass.

What should be her face, isn't.
Instead, an uninhabited hollow — a starveling sidelong glance,
skin
wraithed
by pale opiate.

A mirror-wrought fetch spins liminal, glooms
cryptic —
forsakes her.

iii.

For all the corruption in her body —
she is linen wrapped
& straight-racked under his muslin tight sack
as salt stains
& curves
bead
from sternum
& down leather
strapped by collarbone.

Behind unpapered walls
she is held
& suspended — not heavy & dragging
or veiled by sulphur
but slight,
slight & swinging.

Fully encased in his plaster cast,
she is strung from above for a fortnight —
blood on her bitten lip,
a lick of rain
on a boarded window, her aberrant crack
of light.

iv.

In a spun web or sarcophagus, silk or lithic stone, for three hundred & sixty-five days or none, her solace, a sun-slit sky.

> Saltpetre eyes open to shadow flickers, image flits, then forcefully shut
> after his pry of scrying knife.

In a cocoon of luna moth or star-shroud, she lies or swings there in her hectic flush, tenterhooked & breathless — coughs, seethes.

> Her words tangle in gasp-strangled speech & a bell rings
> & again his voice in the hall recedes.

v.

A faint sheen at first.

Hemorrhaging by half-spoonful heightened to cup.

Until his hypodermic drips a circlet above her wrist — clockwise, he loves her.

~

A mask pulled over mouth slips ether mist as she ten counts back from.

~

Scent of him — discreet & chloroformic
or miasmic, a dark vapouring
through the crack under the surgery's stainless door.

Tremors in her pulse as she is laid out again —
his hands pulling until she is lying along the length of it
& she is looking at a light, a light, a light & nothing is happening above her
& yesterday was lamb's wool under her walking skirt
& wasn't it or weren't they
& didn't she hold a piece of him when she came here
before she slipped listless & antiseptic.

Almandine.

Obsidian with mother-of-pearl.

⁓

Her hands clasp, unclasp.

He leans in & untethers her lungs.

vi.

He palpates —

        here

             &   here

    &   here.

vii.

Brings her laudanum on ice & she presses up against
as he sheet tucks —

he misses her in the morning.

viii.

O Pleasure Gardens of Battersea Park.

O perpetual jones.

O Margate Fair.

O honey.

O Pigalle Club.

O heart's-ease.

O Piccadilly Rooftop.

O syrup of violets.

O Oasis Pool.

O hysteric.

O Great Pretender.

O manna.

O Petit Mort.

O cyanide concoctions applied between layers of warm moist cloth.

ix.

Twists her strait waistcoat
& her wrist

strapped to her hemlock pasteboard pocket flask
until she weakens,

swoons —
a sang-froid somatic apparition

lured
back

through the racket of spinning rooms &
partitioned halls.

x.

Out of the ether with her arms bruised & in restraint.
Back arched black & violet from her last arc of sleep.

Thorax cracked & ribs cut & her tongue-flicked teeth.
Abacus pearls.

Eyes twitch aphasic or semaphoric under his hanging
filament — a grief-rattled lung rasp, proof of a vessel

of pine planks & turpentine perfume. Stripped raw &
ulceric — her night viscera, her white gown split.

xi.

Fresh cat-skin wound around her chest, she is shiver-let from slick wet fur.
Mouth agape & panting, her fingers in-slip his white witch —

vat rendered tallow &
smouldering pitch.

Drop-attacked & camphor-shocked cataleptic, she swallows horehound &
tar feather & cod liver oil.

Good night.

Good night.

Good night.

It's time to go to bed.

xii.

His hand-cupped flame —

then cherry smoke before leaving & her quiet-quiet
tugging at blue ribbons & bandages.

      She unsummons him.

Unsummons her crying room & slat-board window crack,
tainted lake & bramble-shade.

Unsummons the fawn at the side of the road, stun-struck,
jack-lit.

                                        Hind legs buckling.

APOTHECARY

walls, there are walls
in our bones
walls in ruins that lament.

Nicole Brossard

Blood-let

A blunt lancet hit aslant to her wrist held up.
Shun-touched until sleep or syncope.

A blood-let succubus.
She-beast above a cauldron of scalding water.

A husk of blue-veined cocklebur.
He turns her thumbscrew hourglass of sand.

Paraffin & Palm Spilled Salt

A bitter of angelica & artichoke with carbolic strengthens & pacifies her body.
Or sixpence spent brings up a black sweat & blister-pops by tonic & suction cups.

She's not bilious but swollen lymphatic.
Cracked rib cage filled with paraffin & palm spilled salt.

She's undressed & under wraps — O spirewort! O collywobbles!
A rapscallion pins her down.

Posset of Foxglove

Red stripes & white. Buckle-strapped to his humbling chair.
Hoodwinked & gooseflesh bristling.

Her eyes twitch a dream of the tree killer.
Torn holes & poison poured to the roots for a view — trees dying where they grow.
Moon slit slipping in & slipping out of gaunt pine. Star whorl.

Mane whip. Her petticoat in a midden heap.
Foxglove sleep on a merry-go-round behind barbed fences & ivied walls.

Decoction of Sassafras

Throat seized with strychnine & hot sassafras.
Powdered seeds of his humbug tree.

Not bear paws hobbled after a coon-masked dance.
Not bear meat as bear bait.

But rouge spots rubbed into her cheeks by a charlatan panderer.
Thin man with a broken accordion tips his top hat toward her & bows.

Tincture of Mandrake

Black bile & melancholy before a sponge soaked with mandrake.
Or hemlock held over a mouth & nose.

Twilight loosens her body.
Barbiturate release.

Before Cerletti & Bini & the dog-catcher's truck.
A dog roped & current through a frantic heart & sectioned brain.

Trust in me.

Flower Water of Saffron

She swallows saffron & canary wine. A somnolent myth to save her.
Or entreats an iodine salve — ward against skin tap & fat scraped off bone.

She wakes up. A wisp of leaf.
A shrivelled lung.

Lifts her head & weeps.

Wades deep into heavy water & floats her dead man.
Or sinks into his gaping pool.

Unguent of Buckthorn

She's cut-back buckthorn. She's unbidden husk & fallen seed.
She's wormwood. She's beehive & thistle.

She's bramble. She's oak burl.
She's bone-fuse. She's withered branches suspended by chains.

She's nightshade & a numbered grave.

Paste of Bear Paw

Deer throat. Fox claw. Bear paw. Sparrow skull held between fingertips.
Sun-bleached cleft of a white-throated scapula.

How human this — held.

Tender lip split. Blood drips. Cracked sternum & fox claw.
Bear paw. Deer throat. Sun-bleached cleft of a white-throated scapula.

Sparrow skull held between fingertips.

Electuary of Vetch

Forget his dithering at her lych-gate, his pine skittish twitch.
Forget his underbelly scent, his soothing hands.

Forget his collecting jar, net & ether, burn barrel & abandoned shack.

Forget her peck marks & claw bites, pushing wings — wet slur of vetch.
Forget her torn clothes & mud-slung tracks.

~

Seraphim.
Sepulchral angel.

Sweet pea petals fall & press sunlight onto her closed eyes.

Phial of Morphine

He seems nice. No. Not nice. Kind. No. Not kind. Humble. No. Not humble. Meek. No. Not meek. Quiet. No. Not quiet. Reserved. No. Not reserved. Taken aback. No. Not taken aback. Angry.

Yes.

He seems angry.

    ~

He prefers a short skirt against bare leg, a rabbit in her lap,
a tattoo above her right knee.

    ~

Faith in morphine, not god. A long list of lovers, delirious injections,
a sequence of broken glass, car crashes. The air in her room, stale smoke.

Yes.

It was such a nice day — she was right to be wary.

PHANTASMAGORIA

If this is where I must look for you
then this is where I'll find you.

Adrienne Rich

i.

Buzzing overhead : stark-wired : up there : his hanging light scalded
hum : car-struck hind flank : flame-swept stag-horn sumac : lost bee
swarm : burr hole : his scalpel in through a left eye & up to a frontal
lobe : the static arc from the empty chamber of his heart : her house
uphill : her unmade bed.

ii.

Augury of crow before trepanning : or scintilla of cinquefoil : sinew
stretched : before bone burrow : new bit between her teeth : needle in
her upper lip & a second in the vertex of her scalp : until her burnt
tinge of mothball : a locked door : behind : or in the darkness of.

~

A crawl space to a briar patch : if her bed were already empty : when
the worm twisted & twisted under wet gauze : ate all but for her live
flesh : after his footsteps came upstairs.

iii.

Nettle whipped to a muscle twitch & a kick : or her jaw clenched in trismus to a salt-lick blue : until a catatonic hum & a switch clicks & reflects her cornea lacking.

Flit of lid : I lash : I stroke : wet oubliette hole filling in : catacombed where she half-slept : unwatched & bleach-drunk : she : I clasp an ivy strand of hair : a penny from the wall.

Twined : trussed : dilated : light-blinded by the lift of a keyless latch : floor-pressed & false-succour numbed : an incubus susurrates with a red apple & an open palm : she unswallows him.

I in relation to : I in a different way : I in whole or in part : my sugar cube in her mouth keeps his taste away.

iv.

Black-eyed susans : meadows of : no : there was wind & there were
waves of : yes : she remembers a lake : a cold lake : a creek to a lake :
no : it was a runnel of eaves : yes : it was cold under the eaves : no : it
was cold underwater : yes : there were waves upon waves of cold &
she was swimming & she was swimming & she was swimming away
from the shore.

v.

Clamouring bush-blind : bluffed by hush-breath : huffing : his punch-
drunk throat scent : or underside : bear skin : stroked along a cut-line :
unbeckoned : slack-sashed : kneeling with trickles of shame-sweat : or
snail slime : not her lush rustling : but briar-body raw & unsnugged :
clambering unbuttoned : murk stumbling from leg-splayed ferns : lax
bracken : lapsed halothane : halcyon: her chloroform stained summer.

vi.

If lithium brought a calming effect : or if he were not he : if he you
the school director's boy : or if she I tied to hooked beam : if she I &
wrist twists & rope burns : or she I by horse straw : or if you flipped
the matchbook in your hand : if you would have just talked & not
held me down & if she I were not I but you by those ivied walls.

POST-
APOTHECARY

you forget — what is it you forget?

Daphne Marlatt

Weaken : Swoon

Pull closer. The air, wet with skin in your calla lilied room.
On a catafalque, you, gauntling,
acquiesce.

Insubstantial in this dreamscape, this rolling eye of night.
Its gloaming shrouds you whole.

O Ophelia : O Crazy Jane

Willow-straw & wildflowers in sparrow-nested hair, she wakes to feathered moons
& clutches a welt of primrose.

Heat tossed as night sweats. Crux of breastbone
cut &
quivering.

Unribbons her pinafore. She is ready.
She is ready.

Open eyes.
Open palms.

Prick.

Pin-needle threaded with catgut slides through fingertips & beads
blood drip — she pulls each stitch tight.

Closed eyes.
Closed fists.

˷

Rigor. Not rictus. Despite her chest tremens & slash soothed by anodyne. Furled opiate sleep.

In a pall of being under-smothered, fallen by fever therapy. A prairie rose. Pale bud plucked petalless.

Red palimpsest congealing on stone floor — where her scalp split against. Her flinching reoccurs.

~

Sorrow —
lye bleached, one palm line left.

Heart caustic &
deep etched crystalline fingertips.

& who is she now.
& who is she now.

　⁓

She answers coherently but misunderstands the burden of his question.

I'll ask you to set aside how you came here.

Now,
we're here & in this together — how is it you feel so alone?

Back-slapped out of the dank & coming to a clearer state, a blanched calm —
there was a crawl space upstairs.

Current : Calm

Like so.
She cut herself out of her cat-skin.

Wind glistening, heaving. Wet fur & body falling from bone.
All curves — cleft & nerve flesh, pulsing.

                                        Nothing left hidden.

Swims after the luscious — moon-streak on surface,
spilled milk,

wine.

An ache, violet in her lungs. Hands pushing for light — a girl's shadow cast.
Looking down at her.

Water does not grab & hold her under.
It is the depth & the cold & the dark that convinces her to close her hands.

Give in.

Anterograde : Retrograde

Gauze stuffed into her mouth until she is licked awake & wild eyed. Magnolia fawn wrapped in cerecloth curled under a briar patch. Doesn't move. Won't move until the click of a switch for his tonic hum.

Until the blue phase & the sun cracks the horizon of a lake.

Callipers. Wires — ligatured. Bilateral temples of the fraught. How still she lies. Wet furred. Dilated. Her dark longing to hide narcoleptic.

This open ward where he is always watching.

Switch.

                    Spasm.

Moth light.

~

Stone moth cicatrix quivering before flight. Hand clenched. Clinging. Her clasp to night ivy. As her flutter beats for wing-shiver. Strand of hair-feather. Waver heart. Quickening. Blood heat before blind faith in lamplight.

~

The sound a fawn makes.
Have you heard it?

The spasm of her body against the grill of his car.

~

Such quiet or it was stillness.
In bleak streaked fern & speckled thistle, a girl not found for days.

~

Impact.

She says what happened before the event is difficult to recall.   Zero point.
Bright white on the highway & a chronology begins.

Shock attending to its origin.

Concatenation

Summon the body still moving at the edge of the road. Summon lung-song, nocturned breath. Summon howling. Summon her blood-rush, rain shiver. Summon lip throbs, split bitten. Summon figments. Summon fractures. Summon sleep.

Summon salved wounds, wings.

A room-burst of white-throated sparrows.

~

How still she lies.

Hush-rapt. Wet furred. Wild-eyed.
Her hollow clavicle heaving where his tongue disgraced.

How skin glistens in glimmer-light.
Flank lashed.

How she shifts to her slick pale body.
Luna moth moult.

Her sutured poet-mouth & wing-bud shoulder blades.

~

Leech welt.
Snake weal.

Under fern crouched. Stricken.
Creased cheeks from lying without sleep. Clenched fists & common crying.

⁓

A cabin window where her moth traced, my mouth.
Pressed against the glass & breathing.

Coveting our sibylant hiss.

⁓

Shore tilt.
Marsh wisp.

Such thirst after swallowed dirt.

Blood-sucker. Sap-licker. Shape-shifter.
She clings to stump clefts, beehives & swollen nests.

Plunge

Sparrow feathers & wing-buds flatten & press
into the forest floor. So be it.

Fall where I fall
& lay back — rabid & frothing.

Face turned upwards, sun-swept.

Or plunge into his thicket snatch, as simple as my frock slips,
as roots claw into earth.

Who could stay like that — above me & hovering
unmerciful.

After murmurs of hush-hush, his gentle stroke
of dark against stigmatic sky.

Untether : Unhinge

Tremulous.
My body taken by its shaking.

Fever blushed.
Touched at the curve of collarbone.

How human this.

Bunting wrapped in rabbit skin. Wind singing.
Meek-swung.

A blue ribbon drawn tight around a wound.

Lips pressed to my pulse
& restless.

Restrain the Body : Rest the Mind

Half-light. Laid down gentle in an alcove. Thorn-slash.
I will. I will not. Sheet clutch.

Unhoused by an upwelled lip quaver — pushing under
& out of air. When white is not white but blue-blue.

Mouth covered by his hands. Red-handed & disarrayed.
His quiet humming & furtive rush.

Wounds : Sutures

Darkness against a window & slipping under sill — I want to lean out & be rain wet,
wash scars from where his fingers crept, sulphuric, until my fever broke.

Would I tell him about her smooth pale body? Skinned cat standing upright,
balancing a tray of emptied teacups, spilled tea.

Four feet tall I thought, with her white tongue lolling.

I am breathing on my own but my fears are blunted flat. Or, inappropriate.
Better to lean out over a basin. Bend & drip water down.

Wash his chokecherry stain from my lip-seam. Suture ripped.
Self-split. Sanguinous.

Would I tell him this —
all my shadows crouch in corners, glisten moonlight.

Clutch. Tear. Disgorge.
A scalp-vein needle taped to the back of my hand.

Yes. I am breathing on my own.
On my own.

EPILOGUE

I thought I heard a girl's voice in the woods. I thought I heard a girl's voice in the woods.

CLINICAL
NOTE

at night, especially at night, it is always at night,
a wall of concrete enclosed me,
it was impossible to open my eyes.

Dionne Brand

Patient was given methedrine 10 mg IV. Before the injection, possible effects were explained & patient consented. In a short period of time, patient broke into tears. She became apprehensive after this & stated I had better call the orderlies because she was going to punch me in the jaw. Through the interview she alternated between crying spells & manic states. At first she claimed I was not going to get her to talk. When she did start talking, she said: Get a hold of yourself Ridley. You have got to get a hold of yourself. *When asked what is wrong, the patient stated she is happy.*

I am happy.

Notes

First epigraph
Denise Levertov, "Claritas," *O Taste And See*. A New Directions Book, 1964.

Second epigraph
Nicole Brossard, "Blue Float of Days," *Notebook of Roses and Civilization*.
Translated by Robert Majzels and Erín Moure. Coach House Press, 2007.

Third epigraph
Adrienne Rich, "Modotti," *Midnight Salvage*. W. W. Norton & Company,
1999.

Fourth epigraph
Daphne Marlatt, *The Given*. McClelland & Stewart, 2008.

Fifth epigraph
Dionne Brand, "Ossuary 1," *Ossuaries*. McClelland & Stewart, 2010.

Acknowledgements

Praise for Cameron Anstee of Apt. 9 Press for publishing "Rest Cure" in hand-stitched chapbook form, and for the equally tireless editors and teams with 1cent, above/ground press, AngelHousePress, *barely their, branch*, cartywheel press, *CV2*, *Descant*, experiment-o.com, *Grain*, NationalPoetryMonth.ca, *RAMPIKE* and *This Magazine*. And also for The Canada Council for the Arts, The Ontario Arts Council and The City of Ottawa for writing time and, especially, for their continued support of the arts.

~

Joy for Amanda Earl, Bill Poock (groundskeeper at Saskatchewan Hospital) for his private tour, Carmel Purkis, Christine McNair for Chiropteras, Emma Lake's Summer Colony of 2008, Grant Wilkins, Jennifer Londry for cordial and candelas, Jennifer Still for nasturtiums on my tongue, jwcurry, Marcus McCann, Michael Blouin, michèle provost, Michelle Desbarats, Pearl Pirie, Peter Richardson, Phil Hall, rob mclennan, Roland Prevost, Steven Heighton for his *phial* of goodness, Stuart Ross, Su Rogers and Tackaberry Lake's Minor Horde of the Disenchanted: Eric Slankis, Nietzsche and Sylvia Barons.

~

For Beth Follett, always, gratitude.

Sandra Ridley has received the bpNichol Chapbook Award and the Alfred G. Bailey Prize, and was a finalist for the Robert Kroetsch Award for Innovative Poetry. Her first book of poetry, *Fallout* (Hagios Press) won the 2010 Saskatchewan Book Award for Publishing. She lives in Ottawa, Ontario.